A Better Way!

The *Break Down Better* Guided Journal

VIVIAN G. CUMINS

All Scripture quotations, unless otherwise indicated, are taken from the Holy Bible, New International Version®, NIV®. Copyright ©1973, 1978, 1984, 2011 by Biblica, Inc.™ Used by permission of Zondervan. All rights reserved worldwide. www.zondervan.com. The "NIV" and "New International Version" are trademarks registered in the United States Patent and Trademark Office by Biblica, Inc.™

The author has added italics to Scripture quotations for emphasis.

ISBN 979-8-218-87666-1 (paperback)

Cover and interior design by Shonda Ramsey: shondaramsey.com

Printed in the United States of America First Edition 2025

10 9 8 7 6 5 4 3 2 1

123025

Contents

Welcome to *A Better Way!*

Introduction

If you are holding this guided journal, chances are you are tired. Not just physically, but *soul tired*—weary from a life consumed by worry, burnout, busyness, and endless to-do lists. Caught between the demands of work and home, maybe you feel buried beneath a pile of good intentions, guilt, unmet expectations, and that gnawing feeling that no matter how much you do, you are still behind.

Perhaps it was the title that caught your attention, because *A Better Way!* sounds like exactly what you need right now—a spark of hope that life can be brighter, more balanced, and filled with joy. Believe me when I say I understand. I know what it is like to be exhausted and run down after years of striving, stressing, rationalizing, and overworking. I have felt the weight of burnout and the crash of a mental breakdown that followed—but more importantly, I have experienced a breakthrough that only God could orchestrate. He not only healed my weary mind and body but also restored my soul by showing me how to live with balance, peace, and purpose.

While I may not know the exact reason you chose this book or what is weighing heavily on your heart, I do know this: You were never meant to live your life stressed, anxious, frustrated, or exhausted. God sees you and your circumstance. He loves you and desires to restore all that has been taken, worn down, or broken. Friend, there truly is *A Better Way!,* and your first step toward that freedom begins right here.

How to Use this Guided Journal

A Better Way! is the companion guide to *Break Down Better: 52 Restoring Devotionals for Burned-Out Women*. While this guided journal can stand alone, pairing it with *Break Down Better* creates a deeper, more meaningful, and transformative journey. It is yours to use in whatever way serves you best, but for the fullest experience, I recommend reading the devotional first and then diving into the guided journal.

In *Break Down Better*, I share Scripture, prayers, and personal stories from my own seasons of burnout and breakdown. Through that experience, I discovered the root of burnout is imbalance, and the way back to wholeness is simple: 1) Keep God first in all things, 2) Care for yourself—body, mind, and spirit, and 3) Have fun and enjoy your life. *A Better Way!* will guide you in putting these into practice and help uncover practical ways to move forward.

Materials Needed

To get the most out of this guided journal, you will need something to write with and a Bible to follow along with the Scriptures. I also recommend pairing it with *Break Down Better: 52 Restoring Devotionals for Burned-Out Women* so you may experience the relatable stories, prayers, and additional Promise Scriptures.

Personal Assessments

At the beginning of each section, you will find a *Personal Assessment*. These assessments are designed to bring awareness, not judgment. There are no right or wrong answers—they are private conversations between you and God. Approach them with openness and courageous honesty.

Each assessment serves as an intentional pause, helping you evaluate your current state so you can more clearly see where God is leading you next. They create a sacred space for reflection, awareness, and growth. By examining your thoughts, emotions, and habits, you gain a better understanding of what is working in your life and what is not.

The goal of these assessments is not self-criticism—it is clarity. These moments of reflection will help you identify areas of imbalance, partner with God to uncover the root causes of burnout, and discover where change or renewal is needed. As you move forward, you will also be able to look back and celebrate your progress.

Scripture to Guide the Way

A daily Scripture is provided to enrich your study, and each corresponds with *Break Down Better*. For a deeper understanding, consider reading the verses before and after the passages for context, and take time to meditate on what God is speaking through His Word. All Scriptures come from the *New International Version* (NIV).

Reflect Along the Way

Each daily entry in *A Better Way!* includes a devotional summary taken from *Break Down Better*, a Scripture, and reflection points to help you pause, invite God into your space, and discern what He wants to reveal to your heart.

The Way I See It

This is a journal prompt. It is your sacred space to respond to the reflection questions and express your honest thoughts, emotions, insights, and revelations that will guide your next steps.

A Better Way! Forward

At the end of this guided journal, you will find a space to capture the "better ways" that you and God discovered together. Think of this as your lifeline—a personal reminder of the growth, healing from burnout, and promises God spoke over you throughout this journey.

Return to it often in the days, weeks, and months ahead. Let it realign your heart when life begins to drift out of balance. Pray over it regularly as you step back into your daily routine, allowing it to anchor you in God's peace and direction.

And when the time comes, do not keep your story to yourself—share it with others. Testify of God's faithfulness and celebrate the restoration He's brought into your life. Your breakthrough may be the spark of hope someone else needs to believe that *A Better Way!* is possible for them too.

On the journey with you,
Vivian

My Commitment to *A Better Way!*

Today, I choose to begin a new journey that leads to peace, balance, and restoration. I recognize that the way I have been living may not be sustainable or aligned with God's best for me. God did not design me to live in stress and burnout. So, with an open heart, I make this commitment:

I commit to surrendering my calendar, to-do lists, plans, and ways to God. I will trust Him to guide my time, energy, and priorities.

I commit to partnering with God to help me recognize the areas of imbalance in my life, and to become more aware of the subtle ways the enemy seeks to steal my peace and pull me off course. When things begin to slip into extremes, I will pause, pray, and allow God to realign me with His truth.

I commit to staying alert and steadfast through God's power at work in me. When I stumble, I will not give up, but will lean into His grace and continue forward, knowing He is faithful to complete the good work He began in me.

I commit to drawing closer to the One who desires for me to live a life of balance, abundance, peace, and freedom. Each day, I will seek God's presence, listen for His voice, and allow His Spirit to renew and restore me from within.

I commit to sharing my story of breakthrough and restoration with others because I know my testimony may be the light someone else needs to find their way out of burnout and into balance.

This is my commitment to *A Better Way!*

Signed: _____

Date: _____

GOD FIRST

But seek first his kingdom and his righteousness,
and all these things will be given to you as well.

Matthew 6:33

When we put God first in our lives, everything else falls into place. Inviting Him into the big moments and the little daily choices opens the door to a life of peace, joy, and balance.

Break Down Better: 52 Restoring Devotionals for Burned-Out Women, Page 19

PERSONAL ASSESSMENT

Read the statements below and annotate which response currently describes you by placing an A=Always, S=Sometimes, or N=Never to the right of each statement. Remember, there are no right or wrong answers. The goal is awareness, not judgment.

I spend intentional time in prayer, worship, or Scripture
each day.   _____

I turn to God first when I feel stressed or overwhelmed.   _____

I regularly surrender my plans to God instead of trying
to control everything.   _____

I am consistent in attending church, Bible study, or being
 part of a faith community.   _____

I invite God into my everyday decisions, not just the big ones. _____

I believe that God cares about my balance and well-being.   _____

I pause often to thank God for blessings, big and small.   _____

I measure my worth by God's truth, not by the
world's standards of success.   _____

I spend more time in God's Word than on social media,
news, or entertainment.   _____

I trust God and live with peace rather than worry and striving. _____

Reflect Along the Way

1. Which of these statements reflect where you are thriving in your walk with God, and which reveal areas He may be inviting you to realign and restore balance?

2. Complete this sentence: "Prioritizing God in my life brings balance because…"

JOURNAL PROMPT

The Way I See It…

_____

_____

_____

_____

_____

_____

_____

_____

_____

_____

_____

_____

_____

_____

_____

_____

_____

_____

_____

_____

_____

Day 1
After a Little While

Scripture to Guide the Way

*And the God of all grace, who called you to his
eternal glory in Christ, after you have suffered a
little while, will himself restore you and make you
strong, firm, and steadfast.*

1 Peter 5:10

G od promises to restore everything that burnout, breakdown,
and imbalance have worn down. While suffering may last
for a little while, God Himself steps in to rebuild, renew, and
strengthen those who return to Him—turning exhaustion into peace
and weariness into steadfast faith.

Reflect Along the Way

1. Thoughtfully consider why you chose this guided journal. How
   have you experienced burnout or breakdown? Journal your story
   below.

2. What does it mean to you that God *Himself* promises to restore you from seasons of burnout and breakdown?

JOURNAL PROMPT

The Way I See It...

_____

_____

_____

_____

_____

_____

_____

_____

_____

_____

_____

_____

_____

_____

_____

Day 2
Hold On

Scripture to Guide the Way

I cling to you; your right hand upholds me.

Psalms 63:8

L ife can feel like a fast-moving merry-go-round, spinning out of control with endless demands, mounting pressure, and unrealistic expectations competing for our attention. In those moments when we feel our grip on life slipping away, we are encouraged to cling to God. His right hand provides the strength to hold on.

Reflect Along the Way

1. In the book *Break Down Better*, Vivian shares a childhood story of losing her grip and being violently thrown from a merry-go-round, illustrating that burnout can weaken our grasp on life. Has your grip started to slip? Has the pressure of work, home, family, and unending responsibilities taken its toll? Journal what is weighing on your heart.

2. How does God's promise to uphold you in His right hand give
   you the strength to hold on?

JOURNAL PROMPT

The Way I See It...

_____

_____

_____

_____

_____

_____

_____

_____

_____

_____

_____

_____

_____

_____

_____

Day 3

All In

Scripture to Guide the Way

If you are willing and obedient, you will eat the
good things of the land.

Isaiah 1:19

Ｔrue obedience means going all in—trusting God completely, even when the path feels uncertain or difficult. When we surrender our will to His will, fear loses its power, and what once looked like breaking becomes the beginning of breakthrough, healing, and divine restoration.

Reflect Along the Way

1. Going "all in" with God means surrendering to His will and being obedient to His direction, no matter the cost. This can be scary! Write out your honest thoughts and feelings regarding obedience to God in this season of your life.

2. God smiles at our willingness and obedience to go "all in" with Him and promises to bless those who step out in faith. Does this promise reshape the way you view obedience? Why or why not?

JOURNAL PROMPT

The Way I See It...

_____

_____

_____

_____

_____

_____

_____

_____

_____

_____

_____

_____

_____

_____

Day 4

Be Fully Committed

Scripture to Guide the Way

*And may your hearts be fully committed to the
LORD our God, to live by His decrees and obey
his commands, as at this time.*

1Kings 8:61

Being fully committed to God means more than momentary enthusiasm. It is a daily choice to keep Him first, even when life gets busy. Commitment shows through consistent devotion, intentional priorities, and faithfulness that endures beyond emotion or convenience.

Reflect Along the Way

1. Is your commitment to God consistent, or does it fade when distractions pile up? Reflect on your answer below.

2. Consider what changes could help your commitment to God stay strong. Write them below and then lift each one to Him in prayer.

JOURNAL PROMPT

The Way I See It…

_____

_____

_____

_____

_____

_____

_____

_____

_____

_____

_____

_____

_____

_____

_____

_____

Day 5

Priority Number One

Scripture to Guide the Way

Dear children, keep yourselves from idols.

1 John 5:21

When blessings or busy schedules take the place of God, our priorities reveal the idols of our hearts. When we return Him to the top of our list, balance begins to be restored, and everything else naturally falls into place.

Reflect Along the Way

1. Take a moment to reflect on how you spend your time, energy, and attention. What do these choices reveal about what matters most to you?

2. Are there priorities in your life that compete with God? Identify and write them down. What shifts could you make that place God at the top of the list?

JOURNAL PROMPT

The Way I See It...

_____

_____

_____

_____

_____

_____

_____

_____

_____

_____

_____

_____

_____

_____

_____

Day 6
Strip Down

Scripture to Guide the Way

Remember how the LORD your God led you all the way in the wilderness these forty years, to humble and test you in order to know what was in your heart, whether or not you would keep his commands.

Deuteronomy 8:2

When God begins to strip away what no longer serves us, it is never to inflict harm—it is to bring healing. In His loving hands, the wilderness becomes a workshop of transformation where He rebuilds our lives stronger, purer, and more aligned with His purpose.

Reflect Along the Way

1. In *Break Down Better*, Vivian shares how she watched her husband completely disassemble and restore his old, rusted high school pickup into a beautifully renewed masterpiece. She writes, *"Looking back, God allowed me to witness that restoration project because He knew I would walk through one of my own."* How does this example affect the way you think about the process of transformation?

2. Invite God to reveal what in your life needs to be stripped away. Journal what He shows you.

JOURNAL PROMPT

The Way I See It…

_____

_____

_____

_____

_____

_____

_____

_____

_____

_____

_____

_____

_____

_____

_____

_____

Day 7

Why God, Why?

Scripture to Guide the Way

> *The weapons we fight with are not the weapons of the world. On the contrary, they have divine power to demolish strongholds. We demolish arguments and every pretension that sets itself up against the knowledge of God, and we take captive every thought to make it obedient to Christ.*
>
> 2 Corinthians 10:4-5

Revelation comes when we stop trying to analyze our pain on our own and invite God into our questions. When we ask Him "why," He reveals the hidden strongholds in our minds and replaces deception with His healing truth.

Reflect Along the Way

1. In a spiritual context, a stronghold is a mindset or belief that opposes God's truth. In *Break Down Better*, Vivian shares that asking "why" revealed a stronghold of perfectionism—leading her to believe her worth and acceptance depended on perfect performance. How does this insight influence the way you view burnout in your own life?

2. What patterns or negative thoughts have you accepted as normal that may be strongholds in your life? Journal them below, then set aside some quiet time and ask God "why."

JOURNAL PROMPT

The Way I See It...

God's Girl

Scripture to Guide the Way

*I have given you authority to trample on snakes
and scorpions and to overcome all the power of
the enemy; nothing will harm you.*

Luke 10:19

As daughters of the King, we are princesses who carry His authority and power over the enemy. Recognizing our identity in Him equips us to stand firm in knowing that nothing can harm us.

Reflect Along the Way

1. In what ways has the enemy attempted to wear you out, distract you, or lead you into extremes such as overworking, striving, or overthinking?

2. What does it mean to you that, as a daughter of the King, you have authority and power over the enemy? How does recognizing your spiritual identity as royalty change the way you view yourself and how you approach burnout?

JOURNAL PROMPT
The Way I See It...

_____

_____

_____

_____

_____

_____

_____

_____

_____

_____

_____

_____

_____

Day 9

Good Morning!

Scripture to Guide the Way

*Very early in the morning, while it was still dark,
Jesus got up, left the house and went off to a
solitary place, where he prayed.*

Mark 1:35

Starting our day with devoted time in God's presence sets the tone for peace, clarity, and purpose. When we dedicate the first hours of our day to Him, He faithfully blesses that time, often returning it to us multiplied!

Reflect Along the Way

1. The Bible is filled with stories of devoted people, including Jesus, who rose early and retreated to a quiet place to spend time with God. Why was it so important that they did this in the morning, before anything else?

2. Write down your morning routine for the past week—include your thoughts, feelings, and actions for each day. Compare your routine to that of Jesus as depicted in today's Scripture. What shifts can you make to allow for quiet time with God in the morning?

JOURNAL PROMPT

The Way I See It…

Day 10

Choose Better

Scripture to Guide the Way

"Martha, Martha," the Lord answered, "you are worried and upset about many things, but few things are needed—or indeed only one. Mary has chosen what is better, and it will not be taken away from her."

Luke 10:41-42

Amidst life's busyness, the most important choice is to pause and recognize Jesus' presence. When we slow down and sit with Him, we experience rest, comfort, and the calm our souls long for.

Reflect Along the Way

1. Martha was anxious and troubled by many tasks, while Mary was focused on Jesus and His teachings. In what ways do you find yourself relating more to Martha than Mary in this season of your life?

2. If Martha came to you, frustrated that Mary was not helping, what advice would you give her? Write it below, then consider how those words might speak to your own heart.

JOURNAL PROMPT

The Way I See It...

_____

_____

_____

_____

_____

_____

_____

_____

_____

_____

_____

_____

_____

_____

_____

Day 11
Faith in Action

Scripture to Guide the Way

In the same way, faith by itself, if it is not accompanied by action, is dead.

James 2:17

Faith is not passive; it requires action. When we actively trust God and follow the steps He calls us to take, we participate in the process of restoration, allowing Him to refine our character and bring about lasting change.

Reflect Along the Way

1. How do you feel right now about having faith and putting it into action? Are you hopeful, hesitant, fearful, or uncertain? Write down your thoughts and emotions.

2. In *Break Down Better*, Vivian provides the following examples to guide readers in putting faith into action. Which speaks to you most, and why?

☐ Thank God daily for the breakthrough, even before you see it.

☐ Guard your thoughts, stay positive and expect that restoration is on the way.

☐ Stay rooted in prayer and Scripture.

☐ Remind yourself that God is doing a good work in you, and your breakthrough is coming.

JOURNAL PROMPT

The Way I See It...

_____

_____

_____

_____

_____

_____

_____

_____

_____

_____

_____

_____

_____

_____

Day 12
Have a Little Talk

Scripture to Guide the Way

Pray continually.

1 Thessalonians 5:17

Prayer is an ongoing conversation with God the Father, Son, and Holy Spirit. It is not confined to formal words or specific moments. Open dialogue invites His direction, wisdom, love, and comfort into our otherwise stressful day.

Reflect Along the Way

1. Reflect upon your prayer life and record your responses to these True or False statements.

   I pray throughout my day. (T/F)
   If it matters to me, it matters to God. (T/F)
   I believe continuous prayer will ease burnout and restore balance in my life. (T/F)

2. In the space provided below, journal the reasoning behind your True or False responses. Then take a moment to share with God what is currently on your mind. He is listening.

JOURNAL PROMPT

The Way I See It...

_____

_____

_____

_____

_____

_____

_____

_____

_____

_____

_____

_____

_____

_____

_____

Day 13

Feeling Froggy

Scripture to Guide the Way

*Do not conform to the pattern of this world, but
be transformed by the renewing of your mind.
Then you will be able to test and approve what
God's will is—is good, pleasing and perfect will.*

Romans 12:2

R enewing our minds with God's truth breaks the cycle of
conformity and chronic stress, giving us discernment of His
will. When we shift our thoughts from the world to Him, we
are transformed, empowered to live intentionally, and can escape the
traps of comfort that harm us.

Reflect Along the Way

1. In *Break Down Better*, Vivian applies the "boiling frog" metaphor
   to describe what happens when we conform to the world and fail
   to recognize danger before it is too late. In what ways have you
   adapted to pressure, busyness, or overwork? Has stress and the
   pace of life increased so gradually that you are no longer sure if
   you are living in alignment with God's best? Explain below.

2. What might the renewal of your mind look like if you surrendered the pressure to perform and let God set your pace?

JOURNAL PROMPT

The Way I See It…

_____

_____

_____

_____

_____

_____

_____

_____

_____

_____

_____

_____

_____

_____

_____

_____

_____

Day 14

Do Me a Favor

Scripture to Guide the Way

Lord, let your ear be attentive to the prayer of this your servant and to the prayer of your servants who delight in revering your name. Give your servant success today by granting him favor in the presence of this man.

Nehemiah 1:11

B old, faith-filled prayers invite God's favor and open the door for restoration, even in the midst of overwhelming circumstances. When we approach Him with confidence and specificity, He delights in answering with love, mercy, and abundant favor.

Reflect Along the Way

1. Read Hebrews 4:16. We are encouraged to approach God's throne with confidence, yet many of us hesitate to ask God for favor because of doubt, guilt, pride, or feelings of unworthiness. What might be holding you back from asking Him for favor?

2. Think about a time when you asked a friend for a favor. Did you trust their willingness to help? How might your relationship with God deepen if you approached Him with the same boldness and trust?

JOURNAL PROMPT
The Way I See It…

_____

_____

_____

_____

_____

_____

_____

_____

_____

_____

_____

_____

_____

_____

_____

_____

Day 15
Fear God, Love People

Scripture to Guide the Way

Am I now trying to win the approval of human beings, or of God? Or am I trying to please people? If I were still trying to please people, I would not be a servant of Christ.

Galatians 1:10

People-pleasing often stems from fear—fear of rejection, disapproval, or not being enough. When our desire to please others outweighs our reverence for God, we become spiritually unbalanced and drained, but prioritizing His approval allows us to serve faithfully and live with integrity.

Reflect Along the Way

1. Why is it important to maintain a reverent awe and respect for God while also showing love to others? How can keeping this balance shape your actions, relationships, and priorities—and protect you from falling into people-pleasing?

2. Thoughtfully consider, based on your actions, whose approval have you been living for—people's or God's? What fears have guided your desire to please others?

JOURNAL PROMPT
The Way I See It…

_____

_____

_____

_____

_____

_____

_____

_____

_____

_____

_____

_____

_____

_____

_____

Day 16
Battle Rattle

Scripture to Guide the Way

*Put on the full armor of God, so that you can take
your stand against the devil's schemes.*

Ephesians 6:11

In battle, soldiers wear armor, called "battle rattle," at all times because their enemy never sleeps. Similarly, spiritual battles are real, and the enemy is always scheming, but God equips us with His full armor so we may stand firm and face every attack fully prepared.

Reflect Along the Way

1. Read Ephesians 6:10-17. Why do you think we are told to "put on" God's armor rather than assume we already have it on? What does this reveal about the importance of daily spiritual preparation?

2. Imagine yourself putting on each piece of God's armor. As you picture yourself fastening each piece, write down how your heart feels. When you picture yourself fully clothed in God's armor, how does it change the way you view burnout and the stress that has weighed you down?

JOURNAL PROMPT
The Way I See It…

_____

_____

_____

_____

_____

_____

_____

_____

_____

_____

_____

_____

_____

_____

_____

Day 17

Built to Withstand

Scripture to Guide the Way

Therefore, everyone who hears these words of mine and puts them into practice is like a wise man who built his house on the rock. The rain came down, the streams rose, and the winds blew and beat against that house; yet it did not fall, because it had its foundation on the rock.

Matthew 7:24-25

A strong foundation in Christ allows us to stand firm when life's storms and pressures threaten to overwhelm us. Just as a house built on solid rock weathers wind, rain, and earthquakes, our lives remain secure and unshaken when anchored in Him. In Him, we can withstand.

Reflect Along the Way

1. In *Break Down Better*, Vivian shares a story of living in Okinawa, Japan, where fierce typhoons and earthquakes tested the strength of her home. The house withstood the elements because it was built with solid concrete and a strong foundation. What might have happened if the home had not been built to endure such force? Similarly, consider the parallels between a physical foundation and Christ as the foundation of your life.

2. In the space below, draw a picture of a house. Label the foundation "Christ." Around the house, write the "storms" or "earthquakes" you are experiencing. Reflect on the house—notice it is still standing? Even surrounded by chaos and danger, with Christ as your foundation, you *can* withstand.

JOURNAL PROMPT
The Way I See It…

_____

_____

_____

_____

_____

_____

_____

_____

_____

_____

_____

_____

_____

_____

SELF-CARE

Do you not know that your bodies are temples of the Holy Spirit, who is in you, whom you have received from God? You are not your own.

1 Corinthians 6:19

Self-care is not selfish. It is an act of worship—a way of honoring and stewarding well the mind, body, and spirit God has entrusted to us.

Break Down Better: 52 Restoring Devotionals for Burned-Out Women, page 55

PERSONAL ASSESSMENT

Read the statements below and annotate which response currently describes you by placing an A=Always, S=Sometimes, or N=Never to the right of each statement. Remember, there are no right or wrong answers. The goal is awareness, not judgment.

I care for my body with nourishment, movement, and rest. _____

I set healthy boundaries and know when to say "no." _____

I resist comparing myself to others. _____

I act on what God calls me to do instead of procrastinating. _____

I ask for help when I need it. _____

I avoid unnecessary conflict and stress. _____

I tend to my emotional health rather than ignoring or pushing past my feelings. _____

I listen to my own needs with compassion instead of always putting myself last. _____

I practice forgiveness toward myself when I fall short. _____

I view self-care as stewardship of the body and mind God has given me, not as selfishness. _____

Reflect Along the Way

1. Which of these reflect the parts of your life that are thriving, and which suggest areas that could benefit from intentional care and realignment?

2. Complete this sentence: "Practicing self-care creates balance because …"

JOURNAL PROMPT

The Way I See It…

_____

_____

_____

_____

_____

_____

_____

_____

_____

_____

_____

_____

_____

_____

_____

_____

Day 18

Dear Me, Love Me

Scripture to Guide the Way

I praise you because I am fearfully and wonderfully made; your works are wonderful, and I know that full well.

Psalms 139:14

Embracing who God created us to be allows us to trade self-criticism for gratitude and grace. When we accept ourselves as His intentional, wonderful creation, we honor the One who designed us in His perfect image.

Reflect Along the Way

1. What personal traits do you view as flaws that might actually reflect God's intentional design in you? How does the way you view yourself affect the balance in your life?

2. Write a letter to yourself listing the traits you admire and those you struggle with, then surrender your perceived flaws and ask God to help you to embrace and see yourself as He does.

JOURNAL PROMPT

The Way I See It…

_____

_____

_____

_____

_____

_____

_____

_____

_____

_____

_____

_____

_____

_____

_____

_____

_____

_____

Day 19
Choose to Live Within

Scripture to Guide the Way

She went and told the man of God, and he said,
Go, sell the oil and pay your debts. You and your
sons can live on what is left.

2 Kings 4:7

Unmanageable debt can quietly steal our peace and create stress, anxiety, and imbalance. God calls us to be wise stewards of His provision.

Reflect Along the Way

1. How does carrying debt affect your emotional, mental, or spiritual well-being?

2. Living within our means honors God's provision. Write down your current financial habits and debts. What areas of your spending or saving could you adjust to align more closely with this principle?

JOURNAL PROMPT
The Way I See It…

_____

_____

_____

_____

_____

_____

_____

_____

_____

_____

_____

_____

_____

_____

_____

_____

Day 20
Stop Looking

Scripture to Guide the Way

*Do not be wise in your own eyes; fear the LORD
and shun evil. This will bring health to your body
and nourishment to your bones.*

Proverbs 3:7-8

L etting go of frantic searching nourishes our whole being.
Allowing God to reveal answers in His perfect timing brings
deep, lasting peace. What we need will come when we stop
looking for it and trust.

Reflect Along the Way

1. How does striving to understand every detail or reason through
   every situation impact your health—body, mind, and spirit?

2. Proverbs 3 reminds us to trust God rather than lean on our own understanding. How could trusting God more and striving less change the way you approach decisions and challenges?

JOURNAL PROMPT

The Way I See It…

_____

_____

_____

_____

_____

_____

_____

_____

_____

_____

_____

_____

_____

_____

_____

_____

Day 21

Apples and Oranges

Scripture to Guide the Way

We have different gifts, according to the grace given to each of us...

Romans 12:6

Comparison robs us of joy and blinds us to the unique gifts God placed within us. When we stop measuring ourselves against others and start embracing our own God-given gifts and talents, we find contentment and purpose in who we are meant to be.

Reflect Along the Way

1. When have you found yourself comparing your abilities, accomplishments, or circumstances to others? How did this affect your peace and joy?

2. Create a list of the gifts God has placed within you. (Unsure? Ask others around you—they know!) Pause and offer thanks for the unique, carefully crafted beauty in each one.

JOURNAL PROMPT

The Way I See It…

_____

_____

_____

_____

_____

_____

_____

_____

_____

_____

_____

_____

_____

_____

_____

_____

_____

_____

Day 22
Called to Order

Scripture to Guide the Way

But everything should be done in a fitting and orderly way.

1 Corinthians 14:40

Clutter and disorder create noise not only around us but within us, fueling stress, anxiety, and mental fatigue. From the very start, God has been a God of order—creating light before land, land before animals, and animals before humanity. Likewise, we too are called to live in order. That was the way it was in the beginning, and it is His desire for us today.

Reflect Along the Way

1. How does living in constant disorder, whether it is a messy space, an overfilled schedule, or unresolved thoughts and feelings, create the perfect conditions for burnout to take hold?

2. Take a moment and assess your physical surroundings. Are there areas where external disorder or clutter might be contributing to internal stress? Write them down. What practical steps can you take to restore order in the areas you identified?

JOURNAL PROMPT
The Way I See It…

_____

_____

_____

_____

_____

_____

_____

_____

_____

_____

_____

_____

_____

_____

_____

_____

_____

Day 23

Sweet Discipline

Scripture to Guide the Way

*For the Spirit God gave us does not make us timid,
but gives us power, love, and self-discipline.*

2 Timothy 1:7

D iscipline is one of the key ingredients to living a balanced life, and one of the most powerful forms of self-care because it preserves God's best for us. Likewise, self-discipline is less about saying no and more about saying yes to what nourishes the body, mind, and soul.

Reflect Along the Way

1. How do you personally view discipline—do you see it as a form of restriction and deprivation, or as a tool for growth and self-care? Explain your answer.

2. In *Break Down Better*, Vivian shares a humorous story about the day she lost all self-discipline and ate every single Christmas cookie herself. What followed was a stomachache, self-loathing, embarrassment, and another trip to the store. Have you ever lacked self-discipline and suffered unwanted consequences? How did that experience make you feel afterward? What might you do differently today?

JOURNAL PROMPT
The Way I See It…

_____

_____

_____

_____

_____

_____

_____

_____

_____

_____

_____

_____

_____

_____

Day 24
Focus on Your Strengths

Scripture to Guide the Way

Do not neglect your gift, which was given you through prophecy when the body of elders laid their hands on you. Be diligent in these matters; give yourself wholly to them, so that everyone may see your progress.

1 Timothy 4:14-15

As part of caring for ourselves, we must intentionally nurture our God-given strengths. When we focus on our shortcomings, discouragement takes root, and imbalance follows. But when we operate in our strengths, we thrive, and it is that visible growth that encourages others to do the same.

Reflect Along the Way

1. List what you believe are your strengths and weaknesses. Circle the ones that you are spending the most time and energy on right now.

2. Based on your responses, how might you nurture and grow your strengths and focus less on your weaknesses? Invite God to guide you in this process.

JOURNAL PROMPT
The Way I See It...

_____

_____

_____

_____

_____

_____

_____

_____

_____

_____

_____

_____

_____

_____

_____

Day 25

The Cost of Peace

Scripture to Guide the Way

Do you see someone who speaks in haste? There
is more hope for a fool than for them.

Proverbs 29:20

There is power in restraint and trusting that God will handle what we cannot. Letting some things go quiets the mind, eases anxiety, and allows space for God's peace to reign. In the end, the calm that comes from self-control is far greater than the fleeting satisfaction of being right.

Reflect Along the Way

1. In *Break Down Better*, Vivian says, "*Sometimes, the greatest act of self-care is the quiet strength of restraint.*" Do you agree with this statement? Why or why not?

2. How can choosing restraint protect your witness, your relationships, and your inner peace?

JOURNAL PROMPT
The Way I See It…

_____

_____

_____

_____

_____

_____

_____

_____

_____

_____

_____

_____

_____

_____

Day 26

Don't Lose It

Scripture to Guide the Way

*Then, because so many people were coming and
going that they did not even have a chance to eat,
he said to them, "Come with me by yourselves to
a quiet place and get some rest."*

Mark 6:31

W e often wear busyness and productivity like badges of honor. We skip vacation and push through fatigue, yet Jesus calls us to rest.

Rest is not optional; it is necessary for renewal and refreshment. Don't lose another day drowning in the daily demands, noise, and distractions—accept Jesus' invitation to a quiet place and breathe, reconnect, and recover from your hard work.

Reflect Along the Way

1. Jesus invited the disciples to *come with Him* to get some rest. Why do you think He wanted to be present with them as they rested?

2. Vacating does not have to be fancy trips or long getaways—it can be as simple as a nature walk. How might you incorporate pockets of rest into your day?

JOURNAL PROMPT

The Way I See It…

_____

_____

_____

_____

_____

_____

_____

_____

_____

_____

_____

_____

_____

_____

_____

_____

Day 27

Let it Out

Scripture to Guide the Way

Evening, morning, and noon, I cry out in distress,
and he hears my voice.

Psalms 55:17

L ament is a God-given way to release our deepest pain, frustration, and confusion directly to Him. It allows us to be honest about our struggles while still trusting in His goodness. Expressing our grief and anger to God does not show a lack of faith; it invites His presence into our suffering and brings emotional, spiritual, and even physical relief. When we let it out, we open the door for healing and the assurance that He sees, hears, and cares for every tear.

Reflect Along the Way

1. Read Matthew 27:46 and Mark 15:34. Both David, in today's Scripture, and Jesus cried out to God in their suffering, asking why He had abandoned them. How does knowing they expressed their pain honestly affect the way you feel about sharing your emotions with God?

2. God invites us to come to Him with our lament. Journal your thoughts, feelings, and emotions in this season. Allow yourself to be raw and honest. God sees and hears you.

JOURNAL PROMPT
The Way I See It…

_____

_____

_____

_____

_____

_____

_____

_____

_____

_____

_____

_____

_____

_____

_____

Day 28

Bless Your Heart

Scripture to Guide the Way

Create in me a pure heart, O God, and renew a
steadfast spirit within me.

Psalms 51:10

Repentance is the key to a heart renewed and freed from the weight of guilt, bitterness, and unprocessed pain. We must be like David in today's Scripture and bring our hidden sins and lingering wounds before God, allowing Him to purify and cleanse our hearts. When we do, we open the door to forgiveness, healing, and the full measure of His blessings. A heart surrendered to God is a heart restored.

Reflect Along the Way

1. In your opinion, how is repenting and asking God to purify (bless) your heart an act of self-care?

2. Can we live a balanced life with unresolved sin and spiritual buildup in our hearts? Why or why not? If you feel led, ask God to search your heart and reveal what needs cleansing.

JOURNAL PROMPT

The Way I See It...

_____

_____

_____

_____

_____

_____

_____

_____

_____

_____

_____

_____

_____

_____

_____

_____

Day 29

Go at Once

And the man who had received five bags of gold went at once and put his money to work and gained five bags more.

Matthew 25:16

P rocrastination can keep us trapped in stress, regret, and missed opportunities. Just as the servant with five talents went at once and multiplied what he was given, we too are encouraged to step forward without delay. When we go at once, the cloud of unfinished business dissipates, and we get to enjoy the rewards of diligent, timely action.

Reflect Along the Way

1. Read the Parable of the Talents in Matthew 25:14-23. How would you describe the servant who received the five bags of gold (talents) and 'went at once'?

2. Why do humans tend to procrastinate? Write down your response, then circle any that resonate with you.

JOURNAL PROMPT

The Way I See It...

_____

_____

_____

_____

_____

_____

_____

_____

_____

_____

_____

_____

_____

_____

_____

_____

Day 30

Strengthen Your Core

Scripture to Guide the Way

For physical training is of some value, but godliness has value for all things, holding promise for both the present life and the life to come.

1 Timothy 4:8

Strengthening our physical core brings balance, stability, and resilience. Strengthening our spiritual core does all of that, and more.

Practices such as prayer, worship, Scripture reading, rest, and obedience not only build spiritual muscle for our own well-being but also empower us to extend compassion and support to others in their time of need.

Reflect Along the Way

1. Ponder today's Scripture. How does focusing on godliness change the way you prioritize your time, energy, and daily choices compared to physical pursuits?

2. List the similarities and differences between physical and spiritual self-care. In what ways might you build more spiritual muscle?

JOURNAL PROMPT

The Way I See It...

_____

_____

_____

_____

_____

_____

_____

_____

_____

_____

_____

_____

_____

_____

_____

Day 31
Time Well Spent

Scripture to Guide the Way

Teach us to number our days, that we may gain a heart of wisdom.

Psalms 90:12

L ike many of us, we often wish for more time in a day, thinking that if we had it, we could finally get things done and find rest. But God has given us the exact hours we need. The key is perspective and alignment. Moses' prayer, reflected in today's Scripture, calls us to recognize life's brevity and to use our time intentionally, focusing on what truly matters.

Reflect Along the Way

1. Do you agree or disagree with this statement from *Break Down Better*, *"The problem is not the amount of time we have. It is how we use it."* Why or why not?

2. Psalms 90:12 asks God to teach us to number our days. What does that mean to you personally, and how does it change the way you prioritize your time?

JOURNAL PROMPT
The Way I See It...

_____

_____

_____

_____

_____

_____

_____

_____

_____

_____

_____

_____

_____

_____

_____

_____

Day 32
Screen Savior

Scripture to Guide the Way

"I have the right to do anything," you say—but not everything is beneficial. "I have the right to do anything"—but I will not be mastered by anything.

1 Corinthians 6:12

While we have the right to do anything, not all things are beneficial.

Technology is a gift from God, yet when left unchecked, it can dominate our days, disrupt sleep, steal focus, and even damage relationships. Setting boundaries around technology, we can reclaim our time, protect our hearts, and use screens in ways that serve rather than control.

Reflect Along the Way

1. 1 Corinthians 6:12 warns against being mastered by anything. How might setting boundaries with technology help in honoring this principle?

2. Rather than scrolling through social media, checking emails, or browsing online, what activities might fill this time in a restorative way? How might that shift help reduce stress, ease anxiety, and support emotional well-being?

JOURNAL PROMPT

The Way I See It...

_____

_____

_____

_____

_____

_____

_____

_____

_____

_____

_____

_____

_____

_____

Day 33

Help Wanted

Scripture to Guide the Way

You and these people who come to you will only wear yourselves out. The work is too heavy for you; you cannot handle it alone.

Exodus 18:18

E ven Moses, the leader of the Israelites, suffered from burnout and needed help. While God equips us for our calling, He also equips others to help us. Delegating and seeking support are wise. Asking for help frees us, opens doors for others to use their gifts, and honors God's plan for community and shared responsibility.

Reflect Along the Way

1. Are delegation and asking for help the same? Why or why not?

2. Delegating certain responsibilities contributes to self-care and balance. In what ways could some of your tasks be delegated to others at home, at work, or in your community?

JOURNAL PROMPT

The Way I See It...

_____

_____

_____

_____

_____

_____

_____

_____

_____

_____

_____

_____

_____

Day 34

Amazing Grace

Scripture to Guide the Way

Brothers and sisters, I do not consider myself yet to have taken hold of it. But one thing I do: Forgetting what is behind and straining toward what is ahead.

Philippians 3:13

Healing from burnout or breakdown takes time and patience. Even the Apostle Paul, one of the greatest voices of faith, admitted he hadn't mastered it all. He struggled, learned, stumbled, and kept going. His progress was not in perfection but in his persistence and grace for himself.

Giving ourselves grace is recognizing that restoration and transformation are part of the journey. Every step forward counts! Keep going!

Reflect Along the Way

1. Think about a time when you extended grace to someone else. How might offering that same kindness to yourself shape your healing from burnout?

2. Write out the following sentence, then read it aloud: *Setbacks do not erase progress. I may not be where I want to be, but I am not where I once was. I have come so far. I will keep going!*

JOURNAL PROMPT

The Way I See It...

_____

_____

_____

_____

_____

_____

_____

_____

_____

_____

_____

_____

_____

_____

FUN

The thief comes only to steal and kill and destroy;
I have come that they may have life, and have it
to the full.

John 10:10

When we laugh, celebrate, and savor the blessings around us, God smiles. Just as a loving father delights in seeing his children play, our Heavenly Father takes pleasure in watching us enjoy the lives given us.

Break Down Better: 52 Restoring Devotionals for Burned-Out Women, page 91

PERSONAL ASSESSMENT

Read the statements below and annotate which response currently describes you by placing an A=Always, S=Sometimes, or N=Never to the right of each statement. Remember, there are no right or wrong answers. The goal is awareness, not judgment.

I make time for leisure, hobbies, and joy-filled activities. _____

I allow myself to delight in simple pleasures without guilt. _____

I laugh often and welcome moments of lightness. _____

I plan and look forward to things that bring me joy (not just responsibilities). _____

I give myself permission to rest AND play. _____

I notice and appreciate fun moments in daily life, even small ones. _____

I create intentional time for fun instead of waiting for "when life slows down." _____

I believe God delights in my joy and created me to have fun in healthy, life-giving ways. _____

I make efforts to welcome others into my home and life, cultivating warmth and community. _____

I delight in my spouse/family; I nurture our connection and spend quality time with them. _____

Reflect Along the Way

1. Which of these reflect the parts of your life that are thriving, and which suggest spaces that could benefit from intentional care and realignment?

2. Complete this sentence: "Having Fun fosters balance because …"

JOURNAL PROMPT

The Way I See It…

_____

_____

_____

_____

_____

_____

_____

_____

_____

_____

_____

_____

_____

_____

_____

_____

_____

Day 35
Do It Anyway

Scripture to Guide the Way

Rejoice in the Lord always. I will say it again: Rejoice!

Philippians 4:4

C hoosing joy isn't always easy. There are days when laughter feels out of reach and fun seems like another task. The Lord delights in seeing us enjoy the lives given to us. When joy feels hard and having fun seems cumbersome, choose to do it anyway. Your soul will thank you.

Reflect Along the Way

1. Read John 10:10. How does this verse shape your understanding of the Lord's heart for you to enjoy your life? In what ways might embracing joy, fun, and moments of delight be part of living the full life He promises?

2. Journal five things that bring you joy and why you enjoy them (family, a hobby, a special treat, an activity, etc.). What small, practical step could you take this week to choose to experience the joy these things bring?

JOURNAL PROMPT
The Way I See It...

_____

_____

_____

_____

_____

_____

_____

_____

_____

_____

_____

_____

_____

_____

_____

_____

_____

Day 36
Laugh Out Loud

Scripture to Guide the Way

A cheerful heart is good medicine, but a crushed spirit dries up the bones.

Proverbs 17:22

When was the last time you enjoyed a good old-fashioned belly laugh?

Studies show that laughing releases endorphins—those "feel-good" chemicals that relax tension, boost immunity, and lift our mood. And if that wasn't enough, laughter is contagious and commonly bonds us to one another. Laughter is free. It is fun. And the best part—it is always within reach!

Reflect Along the Way

1. Going back to the opening question, when was the last time you enjoyed a good old-fashioned belly laugh? Think about where you were, who you were with, and what made you laugh. Write down the words that describe your feelings in that moment (relaxed, silly, happy, etc.).

2. Knowing that laughter has real health benefits, does this change how you view or prioritize it in your life? How can you create the space in your day to laugh more often?

JOURNAL PROMPT

The Way I See It...

_____

_____

_____

_____

_____

_____

_____

_____

_____

_____

_____

_____

_____

_____

_____

_____

_____

Day 37
Water the Garden

Scripture to Guide the Way

Awake, north wind, and come, south wind! Blow on my garden, that its fragrance may spread everywhere. Let my beloved come into his garden and taste its choice fruits.

Song of Solomon 4:16

In marriage, intimacy thrives when it is nurtured. Connection, whether spiritual, emotional, or physical, requires attention—just like a garden needs water to survive.

Life's responsibilities and routines can make closeness feel like just another task, but fun and playfulness are essential to keeping marital relationships alive.

Reflect Along the Way

1. What helps you feel most connected to your spouse or significant other?

2. What daily routines or responsibilities tend to get in the way of closeness? How might you "water the garden" this week?

JOURNAL PROMPT

The Way I See It…

_____

_____

_____

_____

_____

_____

_____

_____

_____

_____

_____

_____

_____

_____

_____

_____

_____

_____

Day 38

You're Welcome!

Scripture to Guide the Way

*Do not forget to show hospitality to strangers, for
by so doing some people have shown hospitality
to angels without knowing it.*

Hebrews 13:2

Hospitality is about more than just opening our doors—it is about opening our hearts and creating space for connection, laughter, and community. Whether it is a simple meal, a shared conversation, or time spent together, showing kindness to others can bring unexpected blessings!

Reflect Along the Way

1. Showing hospitality can bring unexpected blessings. How do you currently open your life to others, and where might you create more space for connection?

2. Hospitality does not have to be stressful. What are some ways you can invite others in without creating additional work or pressure on yourself?

JOURNAL PROMPT

The Way I See It...

_____

_____

_____

_____

_____

_____

_____

_____

_____

_____

_____

_____

_____

_____

_____

_____

_____

_____

Day 39
Just Kiddin'

Scripture to Guide the Way

And he said: "Truly I tell you, unless you change and become like little children, you will never enter the kingdom of heaven."

Matthew 18:3

Children are full of giggles, wonder, trust, and joy. They marvel at creation, receive gifts with open hearts, and explore life with curiosity and playfulness. As adults, however, responsibilities, disappointments, and the constant push to keep moving often dull our sense of awe, and we trade imagination for practicality, missing the simple beauty God places around us.

Creation is a gift meant to be savored. From glowing sunsets and rolling ocean waves to buzzing bees and star-filled skies, God invites us to slow down, embrace childlike wonder, and delight in the world He has made.

Reflect Along the Way

1. Jesus said we should become like little children. What qualities of children do you think He meant, and why might it be important for adults to embrace them?

2. How can pausing to marvel, play, and explore bring more fun and balance into your life? In what ways can you bring wonder and awe into your day?

JOURNAL PROMPT

The Way I See It…

_____

_____

_____

_____

_____

_____

_____

_____

_____

_____

_____

_____

_____

_____

_____

_____

Day 40
All Work and No Play

Scripture to Guide the Way

That each of them may eat and drink and find satisfaction in all their toil—this is the gift of God.

Ecclesiastes 3:13

Work is meant to be more than a grind. Approaching work with the right heart can transform daily tasks into opportunities for fulfillment. Joy can be as simple as sharing a laugh with coworkers, humming along to a tune while completing a task, or finding small moments of playfulness in your routine. By embracing service, lightheartedness, and perspective, we can reclaim the gift of work.

Reflect Along the Way

1. Work (paid or unpaid) is often viewed as a burden. But work was originally meant to be joyful and collaborative with God (Genesis 2:15). In your opinion, what has contributed to this shift in how society views work?

2. How do you view your work right now? Does it feel exhausting and draining? What do you think has influenced those feelings? (Stress, expectations, or something else?) What adjustments can be made to bring you joy while you work?

JOURNAL PROMPT
The Way I See It...

_____

_____

_____

_____

_____

_____

_____

_____

_____

_____

_____

_____

_____

_____

_____

_____

_____

Day 41

Blink of An Eye

Scripture to Guide the Way

*Children are a heritage from the LORD, offspring
a reward from him.*

Psalms 127:3

C hildren grow up in the blink of an eye, and moments once held in our arms quickly become memories in the rearview mirror.

Amid life's busyness, it can feel impossible to be fully present, but Jesus shows us the importance of attentiveness and accessibility, welcoming even the smallest ones with love and focus. Being truly present: listening, playing, laughing, and sharing time, honors the gift of children and creates memories that last a lifetime. Presence is free, intentional, and priceless, and it reflects God's heart for those He entrusts to us.

Reflect Along the Way

1. What does the phrase "in the blink of an eye" mean to you? How does this idea apply when you think about the loved ones placed in your life?

2. Parenthood can come in many forms—biological, adoptive, step, spiritual, or even through the love of a pet. It is a gift that busyness should never overshadow. What are some ways to be more present, attentive, or accessible to the children and loved ones in your life?

JOURNAL PROMPT

The Way I See It...

Day 42
Remember When

Scripture to Guide the Way

*I will remember the deeds of the LORD; yes, I
will remember your miracles of long ago.*

Psalms 77:11

Reminiscing about the "good old days" reconnects us to joy,
gratitude, and the moments that shaped who we are. Reflecting
on happy memories, whether childhood adventures, small-
town traditions, or shared laughter with loved ones, can lift our spirits
and bring delight even in difficult seasons.

Reflect Along the Way

1. How does recalling God's faithfulness or past blessings help you
   navigate current challenges?

2. Choose a happy memory and share it with a friend or loved one. Relive the moment and notice how it nourishes your spirit. Journal the experience.

JOURNAL PROMPT

The Way I See It...

_____

_____

_____

_____

_____

_____

_____

_____

_____

_____

_____

_____

_____

_____

_____

_____

Day 43

Encourage Yourself (on Purpose)

Scripture to Guide the Way

But David found strength in the LORD his God.

1 Samuel 30:6

Today's Scripture shows David in the midst of devastating circumstances, yet he refused to sink into despair. Instead, he deliberately encouraged himself in the Lord.

David's example is an excellent reminder that we do not have to wait for external encouragement to feel strength, have fun, or experience happiness. All we have to do is remind ourselves of God's promises and faithfulness, and strength will abound, and joy will return!

Reflect Along the Way

1. Today's Scripture says that David *found* strength in the Lord. The word *found* suggests he looked for it—he was intentional. Why is it so important that we take an active role when we are feeling discouraged, burned out, and overwhelmed?

2. Think back to a time when you offered an encouraging word to someone. What did you say or do? How might you do the same for yourself?

JOURNAL PROMPT

The Way I See It...

_____

_____

_____

_____

_____

_____

_____

_____

_____

_____

_____

_____

_____

_____

_____

_____

_____

_____

Day 44

Happy Endings

Scripture to Guide the Way

*See, the former things have taken place, and new
things I declare...*

Isaiah 42:9

When what once brought us joy begins to feel draining and unfulfilling, it could be God's gentle nudge to let it go. Endings are not meant to leave us empty; they are often openings for new blessings and fresh adventures!

Reflect Along the Way

1. When God closes a door, He often opens another. What opportunities, growth, or blessings might become possible when you lay something down in obedience to Him?

2. How do new opportunities make you feel? Write down your thoughts and ask God to reveal what new things He wants to do in your life, and fill you with the excitement He has for what is ahead.

JOURNAL PROMPT

The Way I See It…

_____

_____

_____

_____

_____

_____

_____

_____

_____

_____

_____

_____

_____

_____

_____

_____

_____

Day 45
Look Forward to It

Scripture to Guide the Way

*Take delight in the LORD, and He will give you
the desires of your heart.*

Psalms 37:4

S
ometimes the desires of our hearts seem far away. What do we
do when God plants a dream within us that hasn't yet come to
fruition? We look forward to it!

While in the waiting room, we can look ahead with hope,
anticipation, and excitement, and use that time to learn, train, pray,
and prepare for the day the dream comes to pass.

Reflect Along the Way

1. The Psalmist in today's Scripture encourages us to *delight in the
   Lord, and He will give the desires of our hearts.* What do you
   think it means to delight in the Lord? And how do you see God
   aligning your desires with His when you do?

2. What is your "it"—the thing that excites you and that you cannot stop thinking about? Write about it in the space below.

JOURNAL PROMPT

The Way I See It...

_____

_____

_____

_____

_____

_____

_____

_____

_____

_____

_____

_____

_____

_____

_____

_____

_____

Day 46
Friends in Low Places

Scripture to Guide the Way

*The LORD God said, "It is not good for the man
to be alone."*

Genesis 2:18

We are meant to have friends and be in community. Busyness and burnout may try to isolate and convince us that having friends is optional, but remember, we were never meant to walk this journey alone. Friendship is one of God's sweetest provisions. Make space for meaningful relationships, nurture the friendships God has placed in your life, and trust Him to build new ones where needed.

Reflect Along the Way

1. Why do you think friendship matters to God?

2. When we get busy or are under stress, friendships are often the first thing we neglect. Why do you think that happens? What habits or boundaries could help prioritize fun, friendship, and community during demanding seasons?

JOURNAL PROMPT

The Way I See It...

_____

_____

_____

_____

_____

_____

_____

_____

_____

_____

_____

_____

_____

_____

_____

_____

Day 47

Eat the Fat

Scripture to Guide the Way

Go and enjoy choice food and sweet drinks…

Nehemiah 8:10

W e are invited to fully enjoy provision and blessings without shame or guilt. Just as Nehemiah encouraged the people of Jerusalem to celebrate after completing their work, we too are invited to savor the good moments of life.

Reflect Along the Way

1. Read Nehemiah 8:1-12. The restoration of Jerusalem's walls and gates was a moment of celebration, yet the people wept and were grieved. Why were they so overcome with emotion?

2. How might you celebrate guilt-free the progress made on your restorative journey?

JOURNAL PROMPT

The Way I See It...

_____

_____

_____

_____

_____

_____

_____

_____

_____

_____

_____

_____

_____

_____

_____

_____

_____

Day 48

The Last Laugh

Scripture to Guide the Way

*She is clothed with strength and dignity; she can
laugh at the days to come.*

Proverbs 31:25

The Proverbs 31 woman met the future with strength and grace, fully aware that challenges might be ahead. Rather than succumbing to worry, stress, or the need to control every outcome, she chose to laugh. When we trust in the One who holds our tomorrow, we too face the future with that same confidence.

Reflect Along the Way

1. What causes anxiety or fear about the future for you? How might trusting God's plan allow you to face those areas with confidence instead of worry?

2. Burnout does not get the last laugh—you do! Write about what it means for you to live like the Proverbs 31 woman and celebrate your future and triumph in Christ.

JOURNAL PROMPT

The Way I See It...

_____

_____

_____

_____

_____

_____

_____

_____

_____

_____

_____

_____

_____

_____

_____

_____

_____

Day 49

Enjoy the Ride

Scripture to Guide the Way

Consider it pure joy, my brothers and sisters, whenever you face trials of many kinds, because you know that the testing of your faith produces perseverance.

James 1:2-3

Perseverance is about leaning into challenges, even when fear and uncertainty are louder than our confidence. Do it afraid and enjoy the ride!

Reflect Along the Way

1. In *Break Down Better*, Vivian shares how, even though she was terrified, she chose to enjoy the ride in a stock car at Daytona International Speedway because she trusted the driver. How can you apply the same kind of trust in God for your future and healing from burnout?

2. Stepping into a new season after burnout or breakdown can feel as unknown and scary as speeding around a racetrack. We often worry about slipping back into old patterns that once manifested as burnout. How does today's verse bring you comfort and confidence?

JOURNAL PROMPT
The Way I See It...

_____

_____

_____

_____

_____

_____

_____

_____

_____

_____

_____

_____

_____

_____

_____

_____

_____

Day 50

Arise, Shine, and Smile

Scripture to Guide the Way

Arise, shine, for your light has come, and the glory of the LORD rises upon you.

Isaiah 60:1

A smile is more than an expression; it is a testimony and declaration of restoration and hope. When we emerge from seasons of burnout or struggle, our joy radiates outward, showing others that healing is possible. Let your light shine! Your smile may be exactly what someone else needs to see hope again.

Reflect Along the Way

1. Read Isaiah 60:1-22. How does this passage mirror your own journey of coming out of burnout or breakdown? In what ways have you seen God's glory rise upon you?

2. In what ways can your renewed joy and smile become a testimony of God's faithfulness to those around you?

JOURNAL PROMPT

The Way I See It…

_____

_____

_____

_____

_____

_____

_____

_____

_____

_____

_____

_____

_____

_____

_____

_____

_____

_____

Day 51

Let Freedom Ring

Scripture to Guide the Way

It is for freedom that Christ has set us free. Stand firm, then, and do not let yourselves be burdened again by a yoke of slavery.

Galatians 5:1

The shackles of burnout and the imprisonment of breakdown have no place in our future. Freedom may come at a cost, but the price has been paid. It is time to let freedom ring!

Reflect Along the Way

1. Take a moment and reflect on your restoration journey. How has God set you free? Journal the experience below.

2. In what ways can you commemorate all that God has brought you through?

JOURNAL PROMPT

The Way I See It...

_____

_____

_____

_____

_____

_____

_____

_____

_____

_____

_____

_____

_____

_____

_____

_____

_____

_____

Day 52

Guest of Honor

Scripture to Guide the Way

You prepare a table before me in the presence of my enemies. You anoint my head with oil; my cup overflows.

Psalms 23:5

The banquet table God sets for us is personal and intentional. Stress, burnout, perfectionism, depression, and anxiety have no seat at the table. Adversaries must stand outside and watch as favor, blessing, and abundance pour over us.

Your moment of victory has arrived. The table is prepared, the feast is set, and your place of honor is waiting. Embrace the joy and celebration that are yours.

Reflect Along the Way

1. God loves you. He is proud of you. He wants to honor you. Let Him.

2. Write whatever is on your heart. Reflect. Celebrate. Give thanks. Express your emotions through journaling your words below.

JOURNAL PROMPT

The Way I See It...

_____

_____

_____

_____

_____

_____

_____

_____

_____

_____

_____

_____

_____

_____

_____

_____

_____

A *Better Way!* Forward

You have reached the end of this guided journal, and now this is your moment to pause, look back, and celebrate how far you have come. The pages ahead are designed for you and God to capture what you have learned, let go of, and what you are ready to embrace.

Think of this as a personal reminder of the growth, healing, and promises that have been written over your life during your journey from burnout and breakdown to blessing and breakthrough.

Look Back Before You Move Forward

Take a few quiet moments to revisit your personal assessments, responses to the reflection questions, and journal prompts.

What has changed in your heart or mindset?

What have you released that once kept you heavy or burned out?

What has God revealed about your purpose, priorities, or peace?

My biggest shifts and lessons from this journey:

Remember the Promises

Throughout these pages, God has whispered truths and reminders of His faithfulness.

Which Scriptures or promises strengthened you most?

What truth will you cling to when life begins to feel unbalanced again?

God's promises that sustain me:

Discover Your Better Ways

As you reflect, think about the new rhythms you have formed that bring balance, joy, and calm to your life.

What will you do differently moving forward?

How will you protect your peace and make space for rest, fun, and stillness?

My better ways to live free and balanced:

Create Your Forward Focus

This is your freedom plan for remaining grounded, joyful, and aligned.

What does living better look like for you now?

How will you respond when imbalance or burnout tries to creep back in?

What reminders will help you stay centered and calm?

My vision for a better, balanced life:

Declare It Out Loud

Finish this section with a personal promise, prayer, or statement that sums up your journey and your commitment to live differently from here on out.

My declaration for the journey ahead:

_____

_____

_____

_____

_____

_____

_____

_____

_____

_____

_____

_____

_____

_____

_____

_____

_____

_____

_____

The Way of Salvation

Jesus answered, "I am the way and the truth and the life. No one comes to the Father except through me."

John 14:6

The Way of Salvation

If you have never prayed the prayer of salvation or welcomed the Lord into your heart, I invite you to pray the prayer below and experience the amazing ways He will move in and through your life.

Dear Lord Jesus,

I believe You are the only begotten Son of God who came to earth to be the Savior of the world. By Your death on the cross, You paid the price for my sin so that whoever believes in You will not perish but have everlasting life. I accept Your sacrifice as the full payment for my sins. I confess my sins and ask for Your forgiveness. Please cleanse me and make me Your child. I invite You into my heart and receive You as my Lord and Savior. Thank You for erasing my past and making me a new creation in You. I now receive the gift of Your Holy Spirit, who You have promised will never leave me. In Your precious name, Amen.

For God so loved the world that he gave his one and only Son, that whoever believes in him shall not perish but have eternal life.

John 3:16

About the Author

Vivian G. Cumins is an author, speaker, and the host of the Juggling Life, Finding Balance Podcast, where she ministers to women seeking a balanced life.

A retired career professional with over twenty-six years of service in the United States Air Force and the Forest Service, Vivian draws from a wealth of experiences and a heart for helping others find peace amid life's demands.

Vivian knows firsthand the challenges women face while juggling multiple personal and professional responsibilities. Having walked through her own season of burnout and breakdown, she now shares how partnering with God can bring calm, strength, and joy. With authenticity, warmth, and wisdom, Vivian equips women to honor God, care for themselves, and live a joyful, balanced life.

Vivian is married to her best friend, Eddy, and is the proud bonus mom to two adult children and a Glammy to five grandchildren.

To learn more about Vivian and her mission work, visit her website at viviancumins.com.

www.ingramcontent.com/pod-product-compliance
Lightning Source LLC
Chambersburg PA
CBHW051629120626
46551CB00014B/2003